Simple Machines

What Is a Screw?

By Lloyd G. Douglas

Welcome Books

Children's Press®
A Division of Scholastic Inc.
New York / Toronto / London / Auckland / Sydney
Mexico City / New Delhi / Hong Kong
Danbury, Connecticut

Photo Credits: Cover and pp. 11, 13, 15, 17, 19, 21 (lower left and right) by Cindy Reiman; pp. 5, 7, 9, 21 (upper left and right) by Maura B. McConnell
Contributing Editor: Jennifer Silate
Book Design: Mindy Liu

Library of Congress Cataloging-in-Publication Data

Douglas, Lloyd G.
What is a screw? / by Lloyd G. Douglas.
    p. cm. -- (Simple machines)
  Includes index.
  Summary: Illustrations and text describe different examples of the use
of simple machines known as screws.
  ISBN 0-516-23966-X (library binding) -- ISBN 0-516-24025-0 (paperback)
  1. Screws--Juvenile literature. [1. Screws.] I. Title.

TJ1338 .D68 2002
621.8'82--dc21

                                                    2002001418

Contents

1 Screw   4

2 Pen   10

3 Vise   14

4 New Words   22

5 To Find Out More   23

6 Index   24

7 About the Author   24

This is a **screw**.

A screw is a pole with a **spiral** around it.

5

A **screwdriver** is used to turn the screw.

As the screw turns, it goes into the wall.

Screws help to hold this **shelf** to the wall.

9

Screws are used to hold
many things together.

This pen is held together
by a screw.

10

11

The screw in the pen holds the two ends together.

13

Screws are used for many different things.

This **vise** uses a screw.

The vise moves on a screw.

The vise opens when the **handle** is turned.

The vise holds wood tightly.

The wood can be worked on easily when it is in the vise.

18

Screws are very important **simple machines.**

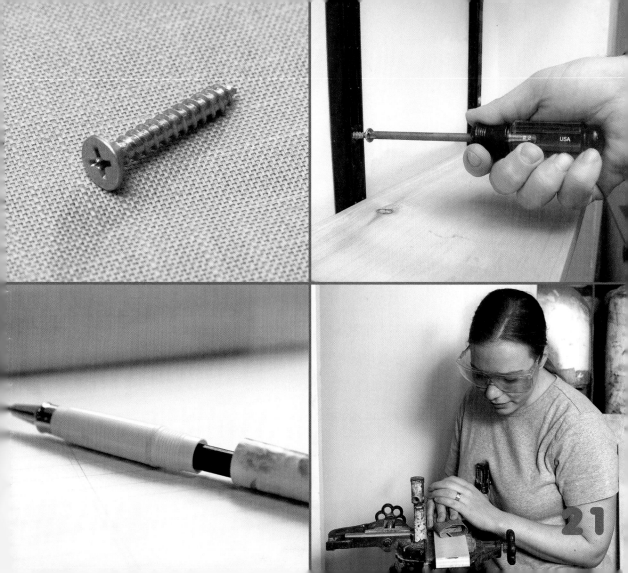

New Words

handle (**han**-duhl) the part of an object that you use to
move that object

screw (**skroo**) a pole with a rim around it, usually made
of metal

screwdriver (**skroo**-drye-vur) a tool with a tip that fits into
the groove in the head of a screw so that you can turn it

shelf (**shelf**) a flat board on a wall used for storing things

simple machines (**sim**-puhl muh-**sheenz**) basic mechanical
devices that make work easier

spiral (**spye**-ruhl) something that winds around in
many circles

vise (**visse**) a device with jaws that open and close with a
screw; it is used to hold an object firmly in place while the
object is being worked on

To Find Out More

Books

Screws
by Anne Welsbacher
Capstone Press

Screws
by Sally M. Walker
Lerner Publishing Group

Web Site
Simple Machines
http://www.mikids.com/Smachines.htm
This Web site has real-life examples of each kind of simple machine
and many fun activities to do.

Index

handle, 16

pen, 10, 12

screwdriver, 6

shelf, 8
simple
machines,
20

spiral, 4

vise, 14, 16,
18

About the Author
Lloyd G. Douglas is an editor and writer of children's books.

Reading Consultants
Kris Flynn, Coordinator, Small School District Literacy, The San Diego County Office of Education

Shelly Forys, Certified Reading Recovery Specialist, W.J. Zahnow Elementary School, Waterloo, IL

Sue McAdams, Former President of the North Texas Reading Council of the IRA, and Early Literacy Consultant, Dallas, TX